In the Dark, Soft Earth

Poetry of Love, Nature, Spirituality, and Dreams

Frank Watson

Plum White Press

For information concerning reprints, email: frankwatsonpoet@gmail.com.

ISBN-13:   978-1-939832-19-1
ISBN-10:   1-939832-19-5
LCCN: 2020903314
BISAC: Poetry / American / General

Cover design by Nelly Murariu at PixBeeDesign.com. Cover background art, "Morning on the Seine in the Rain," by Claude Monet.

Also by Frank Watson

The Dollhouse Mirror
Seas to Mulberries
One Hundred Leaves

Contact

 @FrankWatsonPoet

Email: frankwatsonpoet@gmail.com

www.frankwatsonpoet.com

Table of Contents

finding meaning
in the subtle underpinnings
of this soft earth

In the Dark, Soft Earth

Book One

Within the Weeping Woods

Eleanor Greenfield, "The Promise" (2019)

origins

to the poet
there is a love for beauty
in all its
terrifying forms

in the quiet
stirrings before
the world wakes
when even the night
creatures cease to speak

with distant sands
turned white as flecks
on wild black hair
I follow the Northern Winds
to where the world begins

before Creation
cast in stone
we built this world
on what was sown

since all eternity is rest
why not use this time
to do our best?

chance

why cry
when there is chance
and a path
that will lead you there?

unable to speak
I borrow her country's tongue
to etch the lines
with prints in a maze
from which I cannot return

entangled

upside-down
the world sails forth
through pond water trees

the branches
of her desire
entangle me
wherever I go

those eyes
that capture me
beneath her tangled hair

those eyes that flicker
like sunlit grass between
the fallen leaves

washed over

the river grew
until it washed over
the land

to sink my feet
into the depths of desire—
wet and doomed

where it all began

standing on the cliffs
at the end of the world
we follow the frozen stream

as it winds through
depositing us deep
into the earth
where it all began

afloat

unseen
like an open plea

nameless
as the endless sea

with mist
that floats out wide and free

~

caught
  in a rain drop
    as all the world
      flows out to sea

~

where her hair is
tangled on the shore
of my sand-washed skin

driftwood

floating driftwood
and the shipwreck
of frozen dreams

marked by rocks
awash on shoals—
never known
to mortal souls

burnt like embers
burnt like the sea—
alone in time
and dead to me

Frederick Carl Frieseke, "Nude in a Glade" (1910)

autumn leaves

growing thin
  to the tune
    of falling leaves

like wind
  that whistles
    a melody

      from another time

falling

wailing river
tears

carved
into the banks

as we stumble on
this path, deep

into the unknown

dust

dust in the wind
on the day we parted ways

at dawn the clouds came
welcome as the red earth
she left on my doorstep

bound in forever
wrapped and wound—
an archive of truth
with ancient secrets
beneath the sand

distance

I wait in a crevice of the earth
to sail out on a gentler day

I cannot
measure the dark—
the rock I drop
falls silent to where
there is no sand

her skin
is moonlight on the shores
where I am wrecked
and will not return

maps

this night
I follow the routes
to ancient lands
like a child thrust
in the wandering dust

she wraps me in
a tiny boat
and sets me off to sail
on a journey traced
through ancient maps

her breath
has blown me
across this half
of the waking world

as I sail along
an endless river
in a tiny boat
to the other side

until I'm hidden
within the night
covered in caverns
deep within the earth
where she and I go
on nighttime trysts

continents

sun sailor
sensual sea—
lost eternity

without thought
there is wind—
she carries me
across the continents
of nightly dreams

spinning
into centuries
of cracked earth
with stories told
of continents
that drift apart

stories

sand moved
beneath my feet
soft as a woman's moan

into the night
lit by torchlight
where I wandered into
her somnolent embrace

somewhere down the river
she made a patch of leaves
where we stayed for days
in a slumber, unable to wake—
as satyrs in a dream

in the forest
there was a cry—
she called for me
somewhere under
the owl's eyes
and the wolf's lament

watching

somewhere
in the night
watching me
and watching still

somewhere

somewhere
alone and free

poor
as the wind

lifeless
as the lilting tune

of an Irish melody

Keido Fukushima, "Leaf After Leaf in the Pure Wind"

Leaf After Leaf in the Pure Wind

wind and sea—
the leaves we leave
for future generations

little by little—
the leaves line up
to be lifted by the wind

pure sky—
awakened to the sound
of a single leaf

trees and skies—
the generations grow
from leaf to leaf

running in the wind—
searching for "self"
in the veins of time

water and life—
a drop in the moon's
midnight reflection

moon and sea—
the life force of the Earth's
wandering expression

step-by-step
across the plots
of fertile Earth

circumnavigating
this pent-up globe—
from the smallest insect
to the deepest roots
that burrow in the Earth

Inspired by Keido Fukushima's calligraphy

snow

in the winter
wind and snow
she plays alone as if
she'd stayed at home

she searches the snow
for footprints
and finds the trail
that leads to home

watching by the window
of time's forgotten drift
she dreams of wandering snow
and dances as the shadows shift

Book Two

Between Time and Space

Nicholas Roerich, "Moses the Leader" (1926)

signals

carved wood—
  love letters written
    before the dawn of time

we speak
  in smoke signals
around in circles
  vanishing
to the touch

the rope
  entwines us
and binds us
  hands and feet
as we set sail
  on silver seas

we shape time
  with a chisel
following the lines
  of an afternoon
  eclipse

  she
is a sculpture
  formed
from the lines
  of infinity
laid out to rest
  on the bed
of salvation

adrift

pallid and hollow
we've drifted
through this town
for centuries
and no one's home

her words
strung up
on stranded hair—
blown away
in the winter wind

smoke gun
thoughts in the air—
these words sit silent there

the naked despair
of a people
without courage
who wander
another's land

walking
in breathless prayer
for centuries
without imagination

where flames drive me deep
into the song of sleep
and the narrow road
that carries me off somewhere

time

shifting through the ages
to the sound of her breath

a thousand diamonds
in every movement
of her breathing heart

in time's abyss
when all the burning flames
have been quenched
and no one thirsts for more

these are the tombs
of a thousand years
grown green with the moss
of life's decay

shores of millennia

these rocks
of a million years
and all the fleeting life
that's graced their shores

in a ballet
of sand and sea
we swim to the shore
of sunlit divinity

blood & bones

from another age
of blood and bones
now buried
in the soft earth

I have lived
a hundred lives

and will die
a hundred times more

Nicholas Roerich, "Conjurer" (1943)

ancient lore

he spent
the ancient nights
before a campfire
lighting the walls
with dreams
of the world to come

in history
there is little
but ruined towns
and clouds
that tell a story

moments

that day
the red red firehouse
was set to burn

in and out
time faded like the melody
in a French café

he read
the message in a bottle
twenty years too late

in the orchard
behind the church
we hid from noontime prayers

thousands
of years later
the old men
still tell stories
by the campfire

chains

one eye
half-awake—
the other screams

crying eyes
iron-beaten bones
blood-soaked chains—
we strain, we strain
to break their reign

madman

roundabout and cast afar
a madman among the stars
sealed to fate
in love with hate
he screams in ancient scars

at sea

in the darkness
not even a guiding star
to show the way

sailing toward
the end of the world—
sea monsters
& riddles
& what little we know

in a village
I wait for the rain
so I can melt
into the earth and sea

she will fling my ashes
wherever the cold wind blows
and I shall return
a child, a spirit free

fossils

in two thousand years
they will find an oak fossil
with the lovers' names

haze

opium haze
in a field of poppies—
her mind expands
in ways she did not seek

secrets

she opens
her treasure box
but finds
what she'd prefer
to forget

sunlight broken
into a thousand little sins

wrapped in a spell
I float between the eons
of her eyelashes
as they open
and close

steps

pausing in that
moment of light
between the steps
of now
and imagination

I swim
in the heartbeat
of her words
and hear the melody
of another life

mirror

a doll stares out
the store window
at the little girl
of her dreams

Book Three

Assembly Required

René Magritte, "L'Homme celebre" (1926)

spoken word

fit into a cube
and packed, as is,
into another dimension
where the spoken word
shall never leave

branches

mind
like a branch

reaching
in all directions

stirring the sun
until it burns

blinded
to all perception

jagged edges

the little girl's
ribbons and bows
reflect like glass
in the old
woman's soul

she read
the jagged notes
of her life
that were written on
the early morning sky

watchman's glare

thorns along the stem—
pricked, the petal slips
to rest on jagged stone

blind to the moon
her skin is bare
between the night-born howls
of the watchman's glare

dried dirt
left parched in thirst
along the border fog

among the green leaves
burnt beyond the spring
until imprinted in the ether
where we dissolve—
never again to see our home

particles

tiny epic
of a tiny mind

~

all the dust
that's swept into
the world's wind
and the particle
that is me

~

myself
in millions of particles
sub-particles

dividing, growing
dying endlessly

reborn
to the joy
of another day

segments

I see her
in segments
that make her smile

she smiles at me
like the dew
that washes over
a morning rose

I drink sweet grapes
in a garden of fire
against the weight
of a lovely liar

a truth
that's caught
for a moment
in the net of her
fluttering eyes

string theory

between the day and night
I walk as a shadow
in the light

stars
adrift in dreams
connected
like a lullaby
and held by a string

wandering in a vision
between the cracks
of reality

an invisible string
lifts me through
the lingering mist

where I spin in a world
of memory and desire
just out of reach

held
together
by a
string

René Magritte, "Thee Nudes in an Interior" (1923)

jigsaw theory

jigsaw night
dyed red and blue—
once more she's
back together again

she put the pieces
together one-by-one
but concluded
that this life was nothing
but a jagged edge

born and reborn
burned in deep
daughter of trouble
formed from the particles
of this fleeting life

she slides her problems
into their compartments
but still they get
all tangled up

in half
and half again

section by section
her thoughts
expand and contract

like a beating heart
alone in the forest

motions

I was with her
when she fell

she spoke
in tiny motions
to the tick of a clock

to draw me in
as a cord wound tight
in a spell

that takes me there
unable to talk

the gaps

divided
soft and simple

fallen stars
and broken stones
have turned to sand

and our minds
unable to bridge
the gap

spirits

thirty seconds
and the broken words
of dementia

washing her face
a thousand times
the mask remains in place

she compartmentalizes
until no one is sure
who she is

in another world
she speaks to the spirits
who still remember

and after she is gone
her mask is the only trace

Book Four

Percussion Mind

Pablo Picasso, "Three Musicians" (1921)

rhythms

dreadlock night
in the rhythm of her arms—
we sing the blues

oh, what she does
to me with her
cello strings

in the dark
rhythms of the night
a cricket's cry

here and there
a feather floating
in search of home

pierced by memory
in a play made for
a dreamless world

we sing by the grave
as the woods grow
to cover it all

in this country
made of trees
the music sleeps
between the leaves

colors

sounds play loud
the lights are blurred

a wayward dance
a sideways glance

we speak in colors
words unheard

interlude

shifting lines
shifting space
in notes
on a blue evening
swimming in jazz

these sweet song nights
that sit on the sound
as we simmer around
the pale brick lights
in a ragtime wolf pack
swing-time track

Wassily Kandinsky, "Small Worlds VII" (1922)

jazz notes

jazz notes
blue totes

cold air
and sudden stares

as bebop blew
this ragged zoo

of thin-skinned moats
and sinking boats

until we knew
our time was through

cubism

putting
together

the jazz cube
beat blues

strum
strum

beat
along

on a tired
Wednesday

after-
noon

petals

voice
on a string

petite
falling

from the frost
of drifting clouds

a petal
tied up

in a pretty
white bow

Subway to the Center of the Earth

groaning men
and tracks

of women who know
the carnal gaze

of tattooed jazz
in deep bass

as we're heading down
a heated core

the violent shore
where drumbeats pound

a prophet's sound
that says
      we're
          m
             e
              l
               t
                 ing

down a hole
of earthly flesh

with three stops left

Book Five

A Dance Between the Light

Charles-Amable Lenoir, "A Dance by the Sea"

dance

three ladies dance—
a devil, an angel,
and the one I love

disordered magic
when our lips begin to brush—
how did it get this far?

fluttered lips—
she begins and ends
with a moan

pale as blue fire—
she draws me down
to her ruined town

until it vanishes
into the emptiness
of memory and time

where body
becomes devil
& eyes divine

as she reaches me
slowly

between the lines

duet

what is heaven
without a taste
of hell?

the scene is set
the curtains drawn—
it's time for our duet

it's easy to begin
but harder than sin
to stay until the end

woman of earth
and mountains
clay and fire—
I will stay
through all the seasons

finesse

when finding a mate
you start with finesse
then steal a caress
until you slip into a state
of sweet undress

William James Glackens, "Nude in Green Chair" (1926)

heaven

too many stairs
before the hallway
that leads to heaven

but if those stairs were lovers
I'd be there already

cinnamon

home
   for cookies
and her
   cinnamon
touch

in the baked scent
of her cinnamon kiss
I taste the day
as it begins

woman of raisins
and molasses—
cinnamon-toasted flavors
laced in every lick

I dream of spice
and wake
with a cinnamon flavor
on my lips

coffee

skinny latte
cappuccino skin
whipped cream on her lips

as espresso
swirls me new dreams
in the breaking sun

rumors

rumors heard
from the lips
of seashells

she laughs
at what she knows
to be true

fate

she sat
with Humpty Dumpty
and gave him
a little push
(for such is life)

she points
as everything floats away
and he wears a stupid grin

yesterday she loved him
but now he's too old;
oh, how the little bee
has lost his sting
and now the flower folds

stained glass

to me
the words were like
stained glass
as I listened only
to the music in her voice

each pulse

each pulse begets the night
each kiss engraves
a stone tablet that lives
for a thousand years

I shudder before
the secrets she veils
as I drift along
the path to paradise

Jean Auguste Dominique Ingres, "Grande Odalisque" (1814)

madness

red, red sangria
too sweet for
vampire teeth

full-bodied woman
drunk on the moon—
devil, prisoner to her kiss
I'm doomed

unashamed
she shows the fullness
of her figure
in a night of dreams

raving through
a long night of desire
when all the madness has sunk
into a warm pillow's rest

poison

I lick the poison
that lies between her lips

delirium to the senses
as it seeps in
the breath of paralysis—
this moment
untouched in time

the sweet poison
she slips me
as she leads me to
an eternal dream

magic carpet

light between light
colors mixed in shades
dyed in wild textures

woman of fire
burnt in a village
beyond the sand
beyond the border

caught on a carpet
that carries us off
to foreign lands

water path

alone among the flowers
sleeping beneath the sun
our love's a fallen shower
whose water path has run

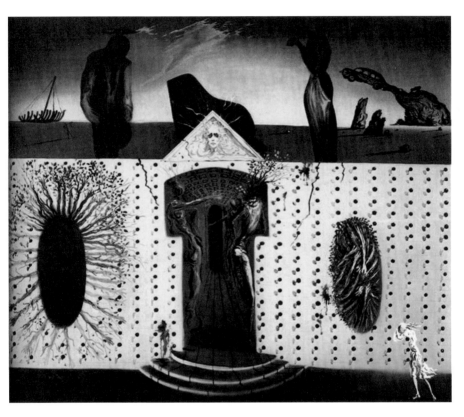

Salvador Dali, "Mad Tristan" (1938-39)

Isolde

she guards the entrance
with a poison-tipped dart

the wind carries her
to a salvation she didn't seek

everywhere she looks
there are more eyes
staring back at her

just a little further
and her prayers will
no longer be needed

Inspired by Salvador Dali's "Mad Tristan"

Tristan

he enters the doorway
like a key that will not fit

he walks the hallway
like the plank on a death ship

he wears breeches
two hundred years too late
but a pretty suit is not enough

darkness enters him
just as he steps through
the revolving door

he carries a shovel
to bury the ones
who didn't survive

the land of nightmares
is so close

he wants to return
but there is no way back
from where he's gone

Inspired by Salvador Dali's "Mad Tristan"

tender flesh

she was a doe
with tender flesh
but the only
ones she loved
were hungry wolves

awash

sea sound
sweet on the lips
of Venus—
a drowning voice
was heard

dew drops
on pine needle tips—
I kiss the tears
she left behind

a cup

she and I
are not the same
and yet . . .
a cup of tea

Is there something
she wants to say?
Her eyes speak
but no sound
escapes her lips.

and then

she hides her prize
so I won't see—
I cover my eyes
and wonder
what's more for me

in the dark
caverns of desire
the lust of her touch
has wrapped me in a fire

of senses interwoven

in the fabric
of thought and touch

where she moves slowly
imperceptibly

like a shadow
toward the act of

completion

Alfred Stevens, "Le Bain" (1867)

late night

the water is warm—
she drifts in the dream
of its embrace

she lies there wet
in soap-stained water
with clothes laid out
for an evening tryst

she exposes
her nude thoughts
to the man who dares
to come close

she paints herself
with the love she longs
to receive

bound

imprisoned
by the golden chain
of unclaimed desire

there was a time
we sought to keep
that promise with
a price too steep

the lock is loose
her feet are free
but she's still here
she'll never flee

alibis

her kiss
has fractured
into a kaleidoscope
of a thousand
tiny alibis

there was one lover
too many in the garden
that would've been Eden

a toast
for her, me,
and the other man

but a crime
is no less a crime
when done
a thousand times

and when she calls
with serpent's tongue
there's nothing
for my soul to redeem

choice

she makes a choice
without a word
as silence sleeps
it's deeply heard

she says
  that maybe
she's after me
  or maybe
the windows
  have shut
and the door
  was always closed

further away

she stares on
as the music carries her
further and further
into the nothing
that lies ahead

shades

nude
she looks
out the window—
her lover's gone
in the early dawn

what she did not say
he knew in the silence
between their lips

silent

she sits there
silent as an owl
with blinking eyes

her eyes

her eyes
are not a funeral
not even the light
that follows the smoke

Book Six

Beneath the Raven Moon

Edward Burne-Jones, "Night" (1870)

she sleeps

she sleeps
beneath the moon
as I slip
into the covers
of imagination

desert of dreams

on a quiet path
beneath the crimson rain

she shadow-walks
across the desert of dreams
to pierce my sleeping mind

etched in ink

whisked to another time
in the pre-dusk hour
when light begins to turn
shade-by-shade
into a nighttime dream

carved
into the woods
in shadows etched in ink—
the night unfolds
on the skulls
of whitewashed lies

night journey

I journey
through the shadows
to join a congress of fire
and melt into
the dream state of desire

dying night

I fell in love
with the dying night
the last drop
of rain's solitude
before the setting moon

beneath the raven moon

barely burning
beneath the raven moon
this frigid night
I wait for you

we kiss in silence
our memories a journey
that ended not long ago

your voice in the leaves
and a name I've carved into
the forest's weeping wood

I ask for nothing more
than a road that never ends

butterflies

these butterflies
on a morning
when all the world
flutters beneath
their wings

on a grass-
scented afternoon
I live my life
in a butterfly's dream

midnight philosophers

the philosopher spun a tune
but his only audience
was the midnight moon

floating in
the midnight smoke
I fade like
the howls of a wolf
on a long, blue night

to moan at the moon
from the dead pool
of collected souls

intricate forest

his beard grows
into a forest
where all the philosophers
can thread
their spinning tales

he builds
an intricate kite
that carries him away

the raven
guides his feet
on a long night
through the forest
of restless sleep

backwoods

one day I got lost
in the backwoods
and decided
never to return

entering
the midnight forest
with wolf eyes lit
to lead the way

the forest curled up
into a story
of stranded souls
away from city lights

shadow wolves
and midnight moons
in a séance of ghosts
that echo a land
we travel only in our sleep

without a kiss

as darkness drinks
the world's light
my eyes begin to drift—
she came into a dream's delight
but left without a kiss

Konstantin Somov, "The Magic Garden (Night Vision)" (1914)

spells

singing to the moon
on this night
of earthly delights

my love for her
was near defeat
but when I fell
it felt complete

beneath her dress
the moonlight rests
in subtle shades
of the spells she made

moon lover

she wades
into the shapely waters
of the setting moon

like golden moons
they bathe in the waters
of each other's reflection

in the forest
of haunted dreams
she closes her eyes
in tranquil sleep

I kiss the water
as she drifts away
but still I see
her shadow remain

drifting nights

a desert night
and all the howls
that lie within
her trembling skin

sleeping from the pleasures
her eyes drift to the mist
of a warm night's dream

it was an empty garden
but the scent of last night's kiss
still lingers in the morning

garden

in the garden of dreams
a little orchid bathes
unseen in the rain

violets
in the midnight scent—
stars in her eyes

a wall within
a wall where all
the secrets grow

in a world of fragments
we piece it together
in the walls we make

hemlock

he is a crow
that nibbles on
the sweet traces
of a hemlock leaf

when the crows
carve their claws
into the electric night
I wake to the caws
of their morning flight

twilight

another layer
in the cold

another forest
in the snow

blinded from
the midday glow

I dance to the sound
of twilight's crow

apparition

my violin is broken—
the strings are twisted
like nerves that scream
a word once spoken

lazier than death
I do not sleep

drifting
in sleepless dreams
I wonder if this
is how reality seems

rolling in a reverie
from one end of the world
to the next
her spirit always
touches me

pastel

on gray and winter nights
I walk the chalky sea
with painted city lights
that drizzle on all who see

the red of night
in midnight lights
has bled into the dreams
of sight and sound

that drift around
till nothing is quite
as it seems

lily

lily in the pond—
I see the reflection
of a girl's smile

lily in the pond
as she floats away

lily floating
among the stars

and halfway to the moon
I kiss my little earth

sunflower seeds

in the downpour—
a smiling face
and a wet kiss

in her mind
I find the sunflower seeds
to my thoughts

that break this night
into a thousand lights
of kissing stars

moonlit ecstasy

in my dreams
I build a castle
where the shadows dance

visions written
in the fading light
of fireflies

kissing her eyelids
in the distant bed
of dried up tears

fancies fall
like fragments
of broken stars

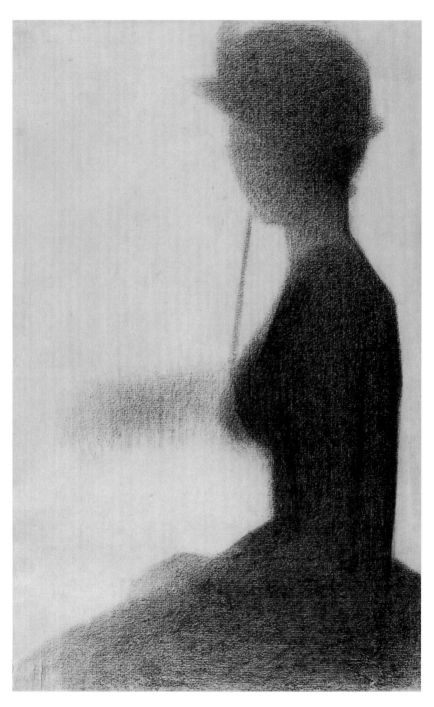

Georges Seurat, "Seated Woman with a Parasol" (1884)

prison of dreams

piercing
the night stars
in a prison of dreams

waking from a daze
she finds herself in another

climbing from
one end of the cosmos
to the other
she never leaves her room

at the end
of a halfway trance
in a labyrinth of sleep

between the worlds

still playing the violin
after all these years
of no one listenin'

the endless earth
where I have grown
with the weeds
and learned from the birds
to fly away free

in this desert
drunk on sand and wind
I am neither man
nor phantom
between the worlds

Book Seven

Omens

Theodor Kittelsen, "Sorgen" (1894-95)

monuments

chiseled
 in marble
stone or dust
 a child of wind
and memory

waiting for her
as the world ends
and all our promises
have fallen from the edge

battlefield

once the field was empty
now soldiers lay strewn—
mist rises in the aftermath
and whistles the sound
of graveyards in the wind

paths

rain drops falling on
the window pane—
she follows
a random path
through an
unforgiving maze

torn in tangles
the bramble litters
the pathway
to what once was

her life entwines
like an ink blot map
and every road leads
to the unknown

old souls

I talk to the dead
with old souls engaged
in a cup of tea

tea

burnt tea served
in a ceremony for ties
that no longer bind

their marriage
was one of afternoon teas
and long silences

sipping
on the leaves
when all our knowledge
is buried in the earth

she speaks
in a whisper as
I reach for her hand

on the edge
of this world
our kisses melt
like tears
in the afterlife

depths

the woods are quiet now
the river broad and deep
these phantoms of my father
still linger in my sleep

flushed in face
hair grown wild
reaching to the ground
while holding up the sky
eyes a demon
and the depths
are far, far below

we rise, briefly
from the abyss of earthly silence
to touch the sunlight
before sinking once more
into the land of shadows
where whispers bring
the echoes of eternity

fog

blind fog
of the senses

outstretched hands
she touches

somewhere alone
where the voice draws her
ever near, away from home

abyss

sleeping alive
in the dark forest
thick with the underbrush of night

her hand is cold
as she leads me to the chamber

the soft silk strands
of her hair fall haphazardly
along the shoulder
as each one lays against
the fabric of her dress

we walk wordless, deeper
into the dark, shrinking
smaller and smaller, until
we disappear into the blue abyss

omens

in the dream scrolls
of the long drawn dead

the water's high
the waves are dark
a flood is coming now
the choice is stark

there were bodies
many bodies
above and below the streets
and all were one with the city

vanished

there was no fish
that day
but even worse
for the fisherman
there was no sea

highs

the city has shadows,
she walks the cobbled streets

gray branches, leaves,
the waste beneath her feet

cold and silent, a siren sounds
and she drowns in a dream too sweet

city

in the city
dark and deep—
the scent of loss
that sleeps within
the ones we meet

lost

dancing in a crowd
the child floats away

walking between the raindrops
she searches for her missing child

the candle burns
and the paper in books
can never explain
what she has lost

John Everett Millais, "Ophelia" (1851)

notes

beside her grave
I left a note
of that time we met
along the riverbank

I laid a lilac
on her plot of earth
and waited
for something new to grow

in the dark, soft earth

on green and broken sod
the trail grows cold
in morning frost

at the bottom of the forest
where I have come to rest at last

so still, the universe
has barely cracked
and the grass stays silent

leaves pile wet
where words have failed

the green turns
hidden in the shade
to seek new roots
among the glades

where I recline
on a hill of fresh cut grass

daisies in the air
the cries of wild birds

and I wait for you
in this life and the next

the stroke grew
through his limbs
in silent death

prayer

on a night
when everyone dances
a lone woman prays

she prays in secret
and somehow, somewhere,
she is heard

for all of heaven
is hearsay
but she listens
to the rocks and wind

reflection

she gazed at me
unable to speak
of her nightmare

I gazed back
unable to speak
as I woke from mine

River Styx

traveler
to the River Styx
without a compass home

warm nights in Hades
drifting beneath the sky

where men perish
and shadows never
cease to call

the rose

the phantom of the rose
has bled through
my unwilling heart
and all the shame is gone

the rose has withered, cracked
and when the arctic wind
brushes down to kiss her lips
she crumbles and blows away

destinations

the spirits have fled
across the sea
and all the gentle voices
have washed ashore

there is time
enough for weeping
as the dust settles
and all the books
remain closed

Book Eight

An Entrance to the Tarot Garden

"The Fool," by Pamela Smith and A. E. Waite, Rider-Waite deck, 1909

fool

he swirls his staff
around the stars—
a wand
on a magical night

because he hides
behind his fool mask
they cannot see
that they are
the greater fools

entranced
by the beauty of a rose
he falls off a cliff
blown only by
the gentle breeze

fire above
and water below—
on solid earth
he welcomes the wind
with open arms

"The Magician," by Bonifacio Bembo, Visconti-Sforza deck, 1441-63

magician

despite the sun
he walks only in
the darkest alleys

he burns two candles—
one for the darkness
and the other for the light

in the butterfly
he sees all the colors
that remain in his life

he knows
his time on Earth
will soon be over
so he plants
a valley of seeds

he places a book on a shelf
to gather dust in the midst
of wisdom's appearance

"The High Priestess," by Bonifacio Bembo, Visconti-Sforza deck, 1441-63

high priestess

she is ancient
as she is young—
and while we look
she stops to listen

she carries her robes
like she has worn them
for three thousand years

her cave is dark
but within it you can see
the entire cosmos

in her eyes, wide-open
I see the dreams
I dare not write

she listens
to the secrets of the night
and smiles
a crescent moon

"The Empress," by Bonifacio Bembo, Visconti-Sforza deck, 1441-63

empress

no matter
where she walks
there is an eagle
watching over her

this night
the moonlit sky
is the only hint
of when the crows
will come out to fly

in her garden
she plants a different flower
for every phase of the moon

because she does not seek
the golden bird
it rests on her branch

"The Emperor," by Bonifacio Bembo, Visconti-Sforza deck, 1441-63

emperor

he had her in checkmate
at the first glance

he reads
the ancient scrolls
and burns them
in the city wreckage

each life
that he has taken
will form a circle
on his walk to eternity

sitting on his throne
he did not
grow his white hair
through innocence

"The Hierophant," by Pamela Smith and A. E. Waite, Rider-Waite deck, 1909

high priest (hierophant)

in the desert
they held a séance
but the spirits
spoke in signs
they could not
understand

with his back to the sun
he is never blind
but his worshippers
will never see the light

he wears a circular hat—
never quite a halo

in stained glass
he sees through the prism
of sewn-up tears

he has never
stopped writing
even in death

and the roots
of his words
have spread
through centuries
of cracked earth

"The Lovers," by Bonifacio Bembo, Visconti-Sforza deck, 1441-63

lovers

darkness brought them together
but light was their only hope

persuaded by
a sudden embrace
and whispered dreams

her dress flows
like an undercurrent
that pulls him
to the darkest depths

running
toward each other
they cannot help
but look
at what's beyond

wounded
he welcomes even more
the soft press flesh
of her embrace

as they sink into the darkness
a malevolent force pulls them deeper

a rose grows
where once she stood—
no matter
how she seeks
she can never go back

long dead
their story lives on
in a torn up scroll
of withered parchment

"The Chariot," by Bonifacio Bembo, Visconti-Sforza deck, 1441-63

chariot

even on
the darkest night
there are stars
to guide her way

with diamonds in the sky
she holds the world between
the dark and light

in the dark waters of night
she keeps warm
with the fire inside

in the wind
she hears the direction
that she must take
for here
is nothing but sorrow

she pieces
the puzzle together
to form a picture
of life in disarray

she plots the battle
like a game of chess
and leads the pawns
to certain death

she drinks
too many stars
and dies by their light

"Strength," by Bonifacio Bembo, Visconti-Sforza deck, 1441-63

strength

he's a lion at her dress
but she tames him
with a sweet caress

she kisses him
before the sun rises
and the field turns into flame

he thinks he caught her
with a lasso
but slips into
his very own noose

in the dance of fire
he always burns out
before her calming waters

on a boat
to another land
she sets her dreams afloat

reading the code
to the whole world
in a single word

in the smoke of incense
she captures the spirit
that fled her first embrace

in time
there is nothing
weaker than strength
but in life
there is a kind of strength
beyond one's death

"The Hermit," by Bonifacio Bembo, Visconti-Sforza deck, 1441-63

hermit

taking his tools
he wanders off
to tinker on a new life

alone tonight
he cups his hands
to catch the lantern's light

he keeps a locket
of her golden hair
to feel some warmth
on the cold nights

rooted to a land
that no man
may ever see

from the summit
he sees all humanity
but misses the nuances

with eyes closed
he knows the way

no longer afraid
he begins the dance
of death

as he draws near the light
his body dissolves
into an energy that flows
throughout the night

"The Wheel of Fortune," by Bonifacio Bembo, Visconti-Sforza deck, 1441-63

fortune

she sets a paper boat
to sail around the world
with a message written only
in her dreams

the words have failed
and she is left
in search of meaning

each step is poison ivy
among the endless paths

in a world of broken gears
she fits the pieces together

~

on earth
we sometimes fly

in wind
we borrow wings

on sea
we sail or drown

and fire fuels it all

but in the pollution
of the elements

we burn

"Justice," by Bonifacio Bembo, Visconti-Sforza deck, 1441-63

justice

her robe is held
by a simple pin
but no one
will pass the sword
that protects
what's underneath

in the black spider web
her justice is darker than sin

she plays the violin
on a night of balanced scales

she holds both
heaven and earth
in one embrace

she signs
her name in stone
forever stamped
upon his skin

on the stairway to death
there is no room
to turn around

in just a minute
it was a lifetime too much

blinded by fire
blinded by night
she breathes in
the cold fury
of faithless pleas

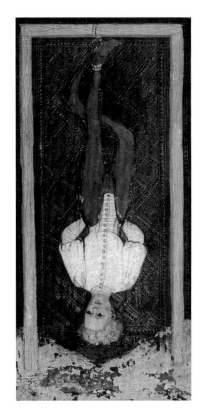

"The Hanged Man," by Bonifacio Bembo, Visconti-Sforza deck, 1441-63

hanged man

it looks like
he will have to take a fall
but the roots he's planted
deep into the earth
will never let go

the paths
to his imprisonment
are many
but the doorway to his escape
is only one

he touches the water
he touches the sky—
between the heavens and the earth
he follows a path
led solely by imagination

on one side is death
on the other is life—
once he thought
there was a choice
but now he knows
that he must wear them both

suspended by a branch
this is the first time
he feels free

in all those dreams
he leaves on earth
upon departing
for heaven

"Death," by Bonifacio Bembo, Visconti-Sforza deck, 1441-63

death

I've died
a thousand times
and yet survived
a thousand more

she comes to me
in the guise of light
but her kiss
is pure night

time is a web
that wraps our dreams
in a spider's bite

joined by a chain
to a fate we cannot see

opening and closing the doors
until life will lend no more

"Temperance," by Pamela Smith and A. E. Waite, Rider-Waite deck, 1909

temperance

in the nude
evanescence
of her curves
she pours me
into a stream
from which
I cannot return

in the wine-dark sea
she drinks the spirits
of another time

each kiss
a potion
that leads her
astray

seeing the world
in so many shades
she no longer senses
the colors of life

"The Devil," by Pamela Smith and A. E. Waite, Rider-Waite deck, 1909

devil

for all the senses
that you may come
to know and desire
he leaves this fruit for you

five corners
to the senses
five shades
to the light
and five phases
to the elements
of body & soul

as the world
turns into rock
he pulls in the sun
to bring about
its fire destruction

stars
have fallen
and all the past
and future
has been laid
upon his head

what you see
is that you are a slave
but what you are
is captured within

"The Tower," by Pamela Smith and A. E. Waite, Rider-Waite deck, 1909

tower

picking up
a thousand pieces—
it comes apart
and back together again

as lightning
lights the path
she falls in time
to heaven's wrath

creation, destruction,
one coin and then another—
searching among the lost
for what there is to recover

we can make it again
a Babel built in tongues—
we can speak it again
when thousands more have sung

burned once more
this life has just begun

"The Star," by Pamela Smith and A. E. Waite, Rider-Waite deck, 1909

star

dreaming of another star
when all I wish
is within the earth

poured in two directions—
I follow the path
that leads to home

planting stars
where dreams are buried

vessel upon vessel—
I drink the cup of life

~

cup of life
poured empty
drip by drip

joining beneath the light
like Adam and Eve
before the Fruit
before Temptation
when all was possible
and man had yet to imagine
the Tree of Life

thoughts connected as a string
to past and present
sand and wind

to eternity
beneath the nighttime heavens
that watch in silence

"The Moon," by Pamela Smith and A. E. Waite, Rider-Waite deck, 1909

moon

in a grotto
where all the spirits lie
the only light
is the light of the moon

lost to the darkness
where the wolf's howl
echoes off the moon—
we drown in the sound
silent in our grief

dropping light
upon the heads
of those who seek

surrounded by
the light of a star
a million years away

each phase
a different face
that fools us
once more

by the light
unable to ask
unable to speak
I reach for the word
in the language of tongues

in a dream
she sails the midnight sea
to follow a path
that only she can see

"The Sun," by Bonifacio Bembo, Visconti-Sforza deck, 1441-63

sun

seeds that grow
in the life force
that surrounds us all
to rise above the earth
only to be buried once more

stones in our steps
built by men
from ancient lands
that rise to the sky
on a sunlit day

walls between us
blocking the sun
yet life still finds a way

dancing by the tree
brought forth
in the radiation of life

hieroglyphics
from ancient times
but the writing
is all the same

"Judgment," by Bonifacio Bembo, Visconti-Sforza deck, 1441-63

judgment

the trumpet sounds
our arms raise up
to the heavens—
no longer controlled
by earthly desire

washing over
as the tides carry
the world away

the angel
has played a song
for all the sinners below—
but how many
will answer her call?

within the rocks
is buried the life force
of the universe
waiting to release
on the final day

alone in our boxes
arms outstretched
for the next phase

a demon has broken free
to wander here on earth
along the crooked streets
to drag the lost to his fiery lair

"The World," by Bonifacio Bembo, Visconti-Sforza deck, 1441-63

194

world

now we've found the wind
and we'll follow it
in threads around the globe
wherever it may go

infinite paths
in the garland of fate—
where *home* is an illusion

there are many paths
she could have walked
and yet the only one
is the one she takes

"Excuse," published by B.P. Grimaud, 1898

Book Nine

Across the Continents

Pieter Bruegel the Elder, "Tower of Babel" (1563)

Little Red Peach

Red as a peach with a smile on her face,
Face with a smile as a peach in her place.
Willow that hangs and shakes its drapery low,
Low is the willow that hangs as wind will flow.
Waves the blossom as wind and hair entwine,
Entwines the hair and wind, this blossom of mine.
Roams the road as the moon sinks west,
West sinks the moon where the road roams best.

Loosely translated from "Bodhisattva," by Liu Dao (1511-1598)

The Phantom Sings

Dancing on the moor
The little creatures
Shaped like dwarves

I drink, and drink some more
Amid the wild grass
The chilling sound
Of children yelling as they play

Who is he? Who is he?
The phantom sings today

Drinking cider, sipping sweet
The spring delights
Of roses blowing
The scent of things undone

White beard, happy belly,
Cup of wine
That dances as I sway

Who is he? Who is he?
The phantom sings today

Little people
Marching through the woods
Telling tales of long lost dead

Give me a mistress
Give me a wife
In love with the sea
In love with the princess I pray

Who is he? Who is he?
The phantom sings today

Inspired by "Le Korandon,"
by Gabriel Vicaire (1848-1900)

red dust

this cauldron carries the mist
of a hundred singing spirits

who wrap around
entwined in a halo

between
the heavens and the earth
the sun and the moon

as we breathe the dust
to inhabit a world
of darkness and light

clinging on
for ten thousand years

dissolved in a drop
an ocean that never ends

Inspired by an anonymous Chinese poem,
"Water Dragon Song" (水龍吟)

the spirits

the spirits
have gone away
but in these ruins
I hear the sacred sound
of the song they sang

楽浪の
国つ御神の
うらさびて
荒れたる都
見れば悲しも

Sasanami no
Kunitsumi-kami no
Ura sabite
Aretaru Miyako
Mireba kanashimo

After Takechi no Kuroto (~700 AD)

Book Ten

Stories Before I Sleep

Henri Rousseau, "The Sleeping Gypsy" (1897)

Witch's Brew

A fern surrounds my life like a hollow maze
In the intricate lattice of love's first gaze;
Following a pattern that guides me on this road
I reach for her lips beneath the mistletoe.

My love comes forth with the apple of desire,
A tangled taste that takes a life to acquire;
Magic and nightshade in a mandrake stew,
I drink the nighttime herbs in a witch's brew.

Seared into my skin like a tattoo of her name,
My cry has faded to a touch without the shame;
Pulled by a thread that stains the earth and sky
Until we're woven in a cloud that blinds the eye.

Awake at once, succumbing to all that's fertile,
Anchored in a moment till we're laid in myrtle.

Plum Garden

They find a garden lush with plum-air scents
As spring sun filters through the dew-dust leaves,
And subtle sighs arise while fruit ferments,
For Eden enters Earth when minds conceive.

Within the garden deep an oak tree grows,
Preserving plum and fruit from sudden squalls
With roots that sink in soil where winds oppose,
To keep the flowers fresh as flurries fall.

Emerging from primordial chaos fair,
This Earth now holds the veins where plum wine flows:
Though autumn atrophies and winter wears
These holy roots renew, reach deep, and grow.

As nothing lies between these fruit-filled trees
So love fulfills with endless mysteries.

For Boris and Miona

sculpture

memory
rolling sand
burnt skin
dried desert
bronze
reclining nudes
modern attitudes
sweet, this sulky you
lying back
curvaceous
luscious brush
shall I draw you too
or shape you through
the desert sand
soft and
will your
skin
last a thousand years?

New York Harbor

leaf and flower
  have fallen in the wind

a petal gone
  the ocean never ends

the sea mist comes
  an unexpected guest

as even now
  the gray moon lingers west

how thin the air
  that blows a subtle scent

my father gone
  the door from which he went

as dust is dry
  it finds its life frontier

but loses track
  a line of song unclear

I stop and feel
  the dead moon's faint reflection

but quiet now
  I walk without direction

within the depths

the Earth is a language
spoken from an abyss

blind, we move our arms, flailing
between the rocks and water

fungus and mold
the coral edges where all is cold

the fishermen rescue us
repair our broken limbs

but there are no victors
there are no survivors

and no one threatens us

anymore

Dave King

in the forest
a bell chimed—
he made a lonely walk

on a rock he sat
and watched the clouds
that passed into the twilight

he followed a stream
and found himself
in a home of warmth

light-colored, the clouds
and night slipped past
the coldness of the moon

she came by the bedside
the angel of night
and kissed his weary head

his final breath had left
for a land of freedom—
she called his name

bones mix with clay
but notes still echo
in the valley of joy

there's nothing to fear
when the clock strikes
and heaven takes us home

*Dave King, a member of the dVerse poetry
community, passed away on October 4, 2013.*

Bohemia

Filling me, the scent
of cedars and pines
along the rocks of centuries,
the beaches of summers
that never cease.

Sometimes soft, sometimes hard,
a dance of water and stone
in the murmur
of soulful woods.

In ancient times,
there were kings and knights,
and endless bloodlines
whose names are now
not even a memory.

I slip between the rays
of speckled radiation,
filtered through the leaves
of the forest's secret places.

Panthers and bears,
the howl of the pack,
alone without armor
beneath a sky of leaves.

I call to my ancestors
who drifted through the forests
and plains of ancient Europe,
filling the abandoned land
with settlements.

In the ancient woods,
it is all a dream,
but this song of the pipe
has never stopped playing.

That Night

That night she died a little,
in a moment before my eyes. I kissed
her and still she did not wake. I lifted
her in my arms and carried her
to an early grave. She invited
me in for a drink but I wasn't ready.
So I walked the nighttime fog and listened
to the moan of her voice for a thousand years.

Island of Song

Afar I row a little boat,
An island of song and show;
Ashore I leave a nighttime note
Of footsteps laid below.

For now it drizzles mist ahead,
Mixed in with dark night green;
I walk a path where willows tread,
A painted river scene.

I open the door and see a room
Of skirts in red and plum;
With girls a-sway and arms abloom,
The beating of a drum.

I watch until my bottle goes,
The noise will leave us soon;
Outside a child unfolds a rose,
Her soul beneath the moon.

Cold Wind

Many years ago, this day,
As lingering clouds
Brought out the morning rays,
I heard the east wind drown
In the sound of the ocean spray.

She came in nightly
On a foaming swell,
Lady floating lightly
On a seaborne shell.

"Oh bury me not
In the deep blue sea;
Oh bury me not
Where the cold wind flees."

I carried her home
For miles and miles—
If only I'd known
It was just for a while.

The words unsaid, undone—
Gone before our time had run.

The whispers ceased
As her lips turned blue
And in the dark distance
A cold raven flew.

For Death has always had his shade
As light begins to fade
In the smoke that's now her face,
A wind that leaves no trace.

Edward Hopper, "Nighthawks" (1942)

Acknowledgements

I wish to thank Andrea H. Gora, Nile Faure-Bryan, Kimberly Lorenz-Copeland, Alexander Nemser, Marissa Waraksa, Jordan Ring, Iain S. Thomas, and Lys Galati for their generous and very helpful roles in bringing this book to light. I would also like to thank my readers, who have given me countless great ideas to explore, helpful feedback, and motivation to keep publishing. Finally, I would like to thank my family and friends for their love and support.

About the Author

Frank Watson was born in Venice, California and now lives in New York. He enjoys literature, art, calligraphy, landscaping, nature, history, jazz, international travel, kickboxing, and powerlifting. Publications include *The Dollhouse Mirror*, *Seas to Mulberries*, and *One Hundred Leaves*. He has also edited several volumes, including *The Poetry Nook Anthology*, *The dVerse Anthology*, *Fragments*, and the *Poetry Nook Journal* vols. 1-5. His work has appeared in various literary journals, anthologies, e-zines, and literary blogs, but most of all, he loves to share his work on social media and in books.

 @FrankWatsonPoet

Web Site: www.frankwatsonpoet.com